More Reading for Pleasure in a Foreign Language

The *Pathfinder* Series

All **Pathfinders** are available through good book suppliers or direct from: **Central Books,** 99 Wallis Rd, London E9 5LN. Tel: 0845 458 9910 (mail order line). Fax: 0845 458 9912. Book trade representation (UK and Ireland): **Broadcast Book Services,** Charter House, 27a London Road, Croydon CR0 2RE. Tel: 020 8681 8949. Fax: 020 8688 0615.

Pathfinder 36
New Edition of Pathfinder 2
A CILT series for language teachers

More reading for pleasure in a foreign language

Ann Swarbrick

CiLT
Centre for Information
on Language Teaching and Research

Acknowledgements

My grateful thanks to the following for their invaluable help in the writing of this Pathfinder:

Hilary Bourdillon, The Open University
Vincent Everett, Fakenham High School and College
Christine Hill, Tonbridge Grammar School
Elizabeth Lazarus, The University of Bristol
Bo Lundahl, University of Malmö
Suzanne McConaghy, Cotham Grammar School
Peter Morris and Heather Morgan, Gordano School
Robin Page, Patchway School
Sally Preece, Stoke Newington School
Margaret Tumber, Renate Lotz, Martine Burgess, Sija Schmidt, Alec Hunter High School

First published 1998
Copyright © 1998 Centre for Information on Language Teaching and Research
ISBN   1 902031 13 X

A catalogue record for this book is available from the British Library
Printed in Great Britain by Copyprint UK Ltd
Typesetting by Gawcott Typesetting, Milton Keynes MK17 9JP

Published by the Centre for Information on Language Teaching and Research,
20 Bedfordbury, Covent Garden, London, WC2N 4LB

CILT Publications are available from: **Central Books,** 99 Wallis Rd, London E9 5LN.
Tel: 0845 458 9910. Fax: 0845 458 9912. Book trade representation (UK and Ireland): **Broadcast Book Services,** Charter House, 27a London Road, Croydon CR0 2RE. Tel: 020 8681 8949.
Fax: 020 8688 0615.

Contents

1.   Introduction

As I sit contemplating this second edition of Pathfinder 2 (*Reading for pleasure in a foreign language*), my thoughts wander back to the writing of that first edition. In 1989 colleagues in the UK had begun to focus on reading again and particularly on how independent reading could potentially be the best means of language development for pupils. Inspiration at the time came from projects in Sweden and Denmark where advances in developing methodology, promoting pupil autonomy through reading for pleasure, were well underway. It is not surprising then, as you will read in this Pathfinder, that that influence has endured. It has also been encouraging to discover that the kind of approaches discussed in the last Pathfinder have been developed by many MFL departments. Some of the examples I have included here have their roots in that work but go far beyond what we had achieved in 1989.

Though many readers found Pathfinder 2 useful, some were critical of its wholly practical focus. This second edition has not lost that. However, in this Pathfinder I have introduced some research-based principles which help to give a clear and up-to-date rationale for classroom-based developments in this area. I have attempted to widen the perspective by including exemplars of different approaches and ways of recording reading attainment from across Europe. The main focus is on pupils aged between eleven and eighteen who experience most of their foreign language learning in the secondary phase of their education. For any MFL department, in the process of developing policy in the area of reading for pleasure, I hope that this Pathfinder provides a good starting point.

A TIGHT FOCUS

Learners will require different reading skills depending on the text or the purpose for reading. We do not read the TV listings page in the same way as instructions for putting together a kit. The latter will require you to read closely for a full understanding of the text while the former will require you to scan the page for particular information which interests you. We can identify different reading skills which a learner will need to develop in order to become an efficient operator in the language.

1. Scanning – running the eye down the page for particular information.

2. Skimming – the same approach, but rather than looking for particular information we are looking for the general gist of a passage.

3 Intensive reading – attempting complete understanding of a text where approximate comprehension will not suffice.

4 Extensive reading – reading for pleasure where we usually neither skim nor scan but read for comprehension of a large amount of text, looking to assimilate the main ideas without always paying close attention to detail.

It is the development of the last, extensive reading, which is the focus of this Pathfinder.

AN OUTLINE OF THIS PATHFINDER

I have divided this Pathfinder into three main areas of interest:

- second language reading research;
- how this might impinge on classroom practice;
- management issues arising from the establishment of a reading programme.

The outline of current research is by no means exhaustive, nor is it meant to be. I have introduced areas of research which serve to give a rationale for the establishment of programmes for reading for pleasure, to give an idea of why I think we should be implementing them and to suggest how this research might influence the planning decisions of MFL departments.

I move the discussion forward by focusing on the classroom to consider what we might do with learners to make the task of reading easier and to give examples from schools where reading for pleasure is planned into the scheme of work. Such a discussion prompts many questions about the management issues arising from setting up a programme of reading for pleasure. I have attempted to ask and answer questions which will be uppermost in the minds of those developing their work in this area.

WHY READING FOR PLEASURE IS IMPORTANT

The aim of extensive reading in the MFL classroom is not primarily to teach language, but rather for learners to use the language they have acquired to understand unfamiliar texts – to give learners large quantities of language input from a variety of written sources. Even in a crowded curriculum there needs to be a place for this.

Donn Byrne, a teacher trainer in English as a foreign language, outlines the importance of reading in terms of its intrinsic usefulness to learners of foreign languages:

- *It offers language learners another area of success. We should accept that not all students will be good speakers and at least give them the credit if they become good readers;*

- *it gives students a skill which they can use on their own;*

- *it is likely to be one of the skills that most students will need in the long term. Certainly it is one that they will always be able to put to use: that is, they can read even if they do not get any opportunity to speak.*

(Byrne, 1988: 46)

READING AS AN EQUAL OPPORTUNITIES ISSUE

Before 1970 speaking in a second language was viewed primarily as an adjunct to written language skills. Over the past decade or so, in UK schools, the tables have turned and the spoken word has gradually taken precedence over the written word. The pendulum swung away from a dependence on the written word for language learning input and study of foreign language texts diminished. The turning point was the introduction of the GCSE in 1985 and the equal weighting of all four language learning skills, and thus an increased emphasis on oral communication. Professor Eric Hawkins, of the University of York, in his address to a CILT conference on grammar teaching, lamented this particular swing of the pendulum and the demise of reading. He pointed to serious equality of opportunity issues in classrooms where teaching and learning emphasised the spoken over the written word. The swimming bath which he alludes to in this extract refers to the need for learners to be immersed in the language either by text or by visiting the medium country – the learner may practise on the side of the pool but will not actually be able to swim until he or she gets into the water:

> *'An implication of this [the demise of reading], which has perhaps gone unnoticed, is that when the written language was the sole object of study, pupils defended themselves with the pen. Their swimming bath was their set books and the library, not across the Channel. It followed that success or failure did not depend, so much as it does now ... on parental encouragement, on the chance to get abroad or to invite foreign visitors into the home. Emphasis on the spoken language has exacerbated the tendency ... for our subject to become more and more a middle class preserve.'* (1993)

His point is important at a time when, certainly in the UK, the need for proficient speakers of other languages is becoming more and more important and languages are no longer the domain of an elite.

READING PROMOTES ACQUISITION

Many developments in the area of reading for pleasure have been influenced by the work of Stephen Krashen and Tracy Terrel from the University of California. In *The natural approach to languages teaching* (1983) their contention is that where learners are 'flooded' with foreign language texts, at an appropriate level and in which they have an interest, they acquire language and that language thus acquired will *'contribute to a general language competence that underlies both spoken and written performance'*. Little, Singleton and Devitt (1989) from Trinity College, Dublin, further argue for the inclusion of many authentic texts in any reading programme because they promote acquisition in challenging learners *'to activate relevant knowledge of the world, of discourse, and of the language system, and thus construct the conditions for further learning'*. All of which points to the fact that extensive reading can produce beneficial effects on pupil learning in terms of developing language competence.

THE AIMS OF A PROGRAMME OF READING FOR PLEASURE

I have pointed already to reasons why reading for pleasure can enrich the school experience of learners. The aims of such a programme differ, depending upon the needs of pupils and the philosophy of the teachers who implement it, but a list of aims might include:

- raising reading standards in MFL;
- offering challenge to pupils;
- developing language awareness;
- drawing pupils into the culture of the medium language;
- creating space in the curriculum for quiet reading;
- developing learner autonomy;
- fostering a love of books;
- exposing pupils to a wide range of texts.

The spin-offs from developing such a programme are likely to be various, but fairly modest outcomes to begin with might include ... for pupils:

- developing an ability to read without help;
- allaying their fears of confronting unknown texts;
- demonstrating that they can achieve without the teacher's intervention;
- learning things they did not know before through the medium of a foreign language;

... and for teachers:

- understanding that intervention is not always the best response;
- developing language skills in pupils which will have pay-offs in other areas of language learning;
- creating quiet time in a crowded week for working with individuals or for reading;
- building bridges between the classroom and the world outside.

2. Focus on second language reading research

There is no hard and fast answer to this question. The answer will lie within the judgement of the teacher introducing extensive reading to his or her class. However, the work of researchers in this area could inform those making such curriculum decisions, hence the discussion of some of this research in the following sections.

WHAT'S INVOLVED IN THE READING PROCESS?

Early work in second language reading assumed that the process was passive, involving the reader in a decoding exercise of reconstructing the writer's meaning through recognising letters and words, making connections between them, building up a meaning for a text from the smallest textual units (letters and words) to larger and larger units (phrases, clauses, sentence links, etc) (Carrell, 1988). So the problem for readers was in effect a decoding problem.

In the late 60s and early 70s understanding about the complex nature of the reading process developed as researchers began to think of reading as an active process and to recognise the importance of the reader's background knowledge. The reader brings much to the text including a knowledge of culture, of the role of punctuation, of print convention, text genre, etc, as well as a less developed knowledge of the foreign language. So there was a realisation that an experienced second language reader could predict meaning by using clues which the text threw up.

Paul Gowan and Maggie Turner (1994) in their research on reading attainment in MFL in Birmingham schools provide us with an example of the use of such background knowledge in the following description of research with pupils in their first year of secondary schooling and their first year of learning French. This is one of the texts they used; it is shown on the opposite page.

They contend that, in order to understand the text, pupils draw on their existing knowledge about the world and about the world of sport in particular, and their knowledge of textual and cultural convention. They describe how they used the text with their pupils:

'At the point where we were working with them, they had reached a unit dealing with "Likes and dislikes", in which leisure activites of various

TENNIS

Boris Becker devient numéro un mondial

L'Allemand Boris Becker a remporté le titre masculin des Internationaux d'Australie de tennis, dimanche 27 janvier, à Melbourne. En finale, le triple champion de Wimbledon a battu en quatre sets (1–6, 6–4, 6–4, 6–4) le Tchécoslovaque Ivan Lendl, tête de série numéro trois et vainqueur des deux éditions précédentes. Becker, vingt-trois ans, a enlevé ainsi son cinquième titre du Grand Chelem. Surtout, cette victoire lui a permis de ravir la place de numéro un mondial au Suédois Stefan Edberg, ce qui était son objectif avoué depuis deux ans.

kinds were featured. The piece was also topical, being drawn from the week's current news, carried by the media both here and abroad. It had all the features which we anticipated would make it readily understandable to the pupils ... Pupils were encouraged to look for words which were the same in French as in English, which were similar to English words, given the context that they were building up, and what they might already know about tennis in general, and this match in particular. As in all areas of activity, some people know more than others, and sometimes the pupil knows more than the teacher! After the pupils had worked in pairs, the results were drawn together in a whole-class discussion, using an OHP version of the original text, on which the teacher underlined the parts of the text which had been understood. This is the version printed. Clearly, pupils had derived the bulk of the meaning from the text ... and had done so under their own efforts, having been carefully prepared by the teacher.'

But there comes a point with more complex texts when the guessing game reaches its limits and false connections, for instance between English and French, impede understanding; when a knowledge of the language is essential.

This brings us back to developments in second language reading theory in the last decade. The Gowan and Turner example above illustrates how the learners brought their prior knowledge to bear and transferred their skills from other reading experiences in order to understand the text. They were playing the 'psycholinguistic guessing game', characterised by Goodman in 1971, in which the reader uses linguistic clues to predict meaning '*and, most important, confirms those predictions by relating them to his or her past experience and knowledge of the language*' (Carrell 1988). In this view of second language reading '*not only is the reader an active participant in the reading process, making predictions and processing information, but everything in the reader's prior experience or background knowledge plays a significant role in the process. In this view not only is the reader's prior linguistic knowledge. . . and level of proficiency in the second language important, but the reader's prior background knowledge of the content area of the text ... as well as the rhetorical structure of the text ... are also important*' (ibid).

This thinking had a profound effect on practice in second language reading. However, more recent research has attempted to show that effective reading requires both strategies (looking at individual words and phrases) **and** using prior knowledge to operate interactively.

So where does this leave us in our discussion of when readers are able efficiently and effectively to begin reading extensively in a foreign language? It makes sense that readers should have a basic knowledge of language in order to be able to process the linguistic information they meet. It may also be that the variety and choice of texts which pupils have at their disposal will affect positively their abilty to read. In other words, if pupils are interested in or have prior knowledge of the content of the text, they will be drawn into reading it. It therefore lies with the teacher to decide at what point learners are ready to begin extensive reading. Given appropriate support, the Gowan and Turner text above suggests that an early beginning can be advantageous in developing reading skills in general, particularly if readers are taught to use all of the devices open to them. So what might the teacher do to ensure the right support for the development of these processes for learners?

WHAT KIND OF SUPPORT CAN BENEFIT LEARNERS?

Before they begin formal mother tongue reading lessons at school, children have typically learned somewhere between 5000–7000 words (Grabe, 1991). By this time they also have an intuitive sense of the grammar of their mother tongue. Second language learners plainly do not have these advantages, but they do have others – their conceptual sense of the world is more highly developed, they have more experience of the world, they have more factual knowledge about it. It is important to make such advantages explicit to learners as they begin reading in a foreign langauge. It is also useful to be explicit about other areas of knowledge which they bring with them as experienced readers of their own language. These areas are very much implicit for many pupils in the transition stage between the primary and secondary phases:

- many will understand the significance of genre, e.g. journalistic register;

- they will have a basic understanding of print convention (that a recipe looks different from a newspaper article);

- they have knowledge of the culture in which they live and this may inform their reading on certain topics;

- they have an awareness of how story is formed (that stories have a beginning, a middle and an end, for example);

- they have a knowledge of basic punctuation and its use as an aid to the reader such as:
  - proper nouns have capital letters;
  - sentences end with full stops;
  - punctuation such as the question mark and exclamation mark aids comprehension;

- they may be aware that many words, particularly in European languages, look similar to English words;

- many know that people read in different ways depending on the purpose (you read a classified ads page differently from a sports article).

Being explicit about prior knowledge can be advantageous to learners. Similarly, it is useful to develop the ability to apply guessing strategies, using all of the clues the text opens up to them, such as those mentioned above, as well as illustrations and typography. In addition to this Rolf Palmberg, in his article in the journal *System* (1987), offers useful advice to teachers:

> '[Learners] should be taught to realise that words may have several meanings, that the morphology of words may be misleading and finally that the meaning of a phrase does not always equal the sum of the meanings of the individual words of which it consists.'

The following example of guided reading sheets was devised by Vincent Everett from Fakenham High School and College in Norfolk, UK. He wanted to develop within learners an awareness of themselves as experienced readers, together with an ability to effectively use textual clues to aid comprehension. His aim was also to raise learners' awareness of what it is to read. In the very title '*How to read in any language*' Everett is suggesting that reading in a foreign language is an achievable task for all learners. He is also encouraging them to see themselves as successful readers rather than strangers to the task.

HOW TO READ IN ANY LANGUAGE

WORKSHEET 1 RECOGNITION

Strategies to help your understanding and give you confidence in reading real materials in another language.

Recognition
- 1. <u>What are you reading?</u>   <u>For example . . .</u>

A Poster   An Advert   A Menu   A Newspaper Article
     A Magazine Article   A Story   Instructions   A Poem
A Diary   Information Leaflet   A Letter   Non-Fiction

If you look up these words in a dictionary, next time you won't need to use English.

- 2. <u>What part are you reading?</u>   <u>Is it ... ?</u>

Complete   The beginning   The middle   The end

- 3. <u>What is it about?</u>   <u>Look for clues in</u> . . .

The Layout   The Pictures and Captions   The Title and Sub-titles
        The Cover   Names of People of Places

- 4. <u>What do you expect? (or suspect!)</u>   <u>Is it ... ?</u>

Long   Short   Easy   Difficult
     Interesting   Boring   Funny   Useful

Look up these words in a dictionary, then next time you won't need to use English.

Check with your teacher now if you are unsure of what your reading is about.

CiLT

WORKSHEET 2 PREDICTION

Strategies to help your understanding and give you confidence in reading real materials in another language.

Prediction
- 1. <u>From your own expertise/knowledge.</u>

What can you say in English about the subject of the reading?

- 2. <u>Language you know</u>

What do you know?
What words do you know in the foreign language which are to do with this subject? Make a list.

- 3. <u>Words you think you'll need to know</u>

What important words do you imagine you will find in a text on this subject? Make a short list and look them up in your dictionary.

- 4. <u>From the diagrams or pictures</u>

Are there any important pictures or diagrams of things you don't know the word for? Make a short list and look them up in your dictionary.

Check with your teacher now if you are unsure of any words

WORKSHEET 3 SECTIONS

Strategies to help your understanding and give you confidence in reading real materials in another language.

Sections
- 1. <u>How many sections is your reading made up of?</u>

- 2. <u>What are these sections like?</u>   For example . . .

| A Few sentences | Pages | Paragraphs | Long | Short |
| Important | | Similar | Lots of different bits | |

Look up some of these words in a dictionary, then next time you won't have to use English.

- 3. <u>What are these sections for?</u>   For example . . .

Instructions	Notes	Addresses	Introduction
Description	Information	Explanation	
Conclusion	Different Examples		

Look up some of these words in a dictionary, then next time you won't have to use English.

- 4. <u>What are theses sections about?</u>   Look for clues in . . .

| Pictures | Diagrams | Titles | Names | Important Words |

Check with a teacher now if you are unsure of how your text can be split up.

WORKSHEET 4 BUILDING UP UNDERSTANDING

Strategies to help your understanding and give you confidence in reading real materials in another language.

Building Up Understanding
- 1. How many words in the reading do you know?

- 2. How many words in the reading can you guess?   Because:
     You know a similar foreign word
          You know a similar English word
               You understand what it's about

- 3. Can you find any other clues?   Look for …

Names   Numbers   Dates   Speech   Questions
     Abbreviations   Punctuation   Brackets   Capitals

- 4. What words are important to look up in the dictionary?
     A mysterious word that appears frequently
          A word you think you recognise but can't remember
               A word you think you can guess but need to check

Make a short list and look them up

- 5. What words is it important to be confident about?
Question words (e.g. What/Where?)   Prepositions (e.g. in/near/on)
Times and Quantities   Articles (e.g. the/a/some)
Pronouns (e.g. he/him/you/it/they)   Conjunctions (e.g. and/but)
Verb forms   Possessives (e.g. my/his)

Your teacher will help you with these, or may choose to focus on one with the whole class.

You should now have read 3 or 4 times looking for different things.

WORKSHEET 5 MAKING SENSE

Strategies to help your understanding and give you confidence in reading real materials in another language.

Making Sense
- 1. What does this reading mean to you?

Choose the words you think suit what you have read, then look them up in a dictionary so you don't have to use English.

Clear	Attractive	Interesting	Informative	Fun
Useful	Funny	Exciting	Confusing	
Dull	Complicated	Nothing New	Easy	Difficult

- 2. Information

What did you understand in your reading? Write a brief summary in English.

- 3. Words

Which words were the key to understanding the meaning? Make a short list and give their English meaning too.

- 4. Reading

Remember you are reading real materials in another language!

Which strategies stop you getting stuck?
Which strategies help you understand most about the reading?
Which strategies make you feel most successful?
What else would you like to be able to do?

REMEMBER TO RECORD YOUR READING ON YOUR RECORD SHEET

IS IT JUST ABOUT READING THE CLUES?

This elaborate guessing game which we require learners to engage in when they meet unfamiliar texts is a high order skill (which many will need to be taught) and is not the only activity which learners engage in during the reading process. In his digest of developments in reading research Grabe (1991) discusses findings from research into eye movements in reading which suggest that '*we typically do not guess or sample texts nor is reading an approximate skill. Rather reading is a very precise and very rapid skill. The reason readers are so fast is not because they guess well but because they can identify the vast majority of words automatically ... identification skills are extremely important for fluent readers*'. It is clear then that developing higher level comprehension and reasoning skills – though important – will not be enough. We need also to include reading strategies which help readers in the decoding process (recognising letters and words and building up meaning from those smallest textual units).

 ## WHAT ARE LEARNERS DOING WHEN THEY READ?

Before considering more activities we might set for learners to become more efficient readers, it may be useful to consider what it is that they do while they are reading. In her research on second language reading Carol Horsenfeld (1984) from the University of California has attempted to uncover the kinds of strategies learners use when confronted with an unfamilair text. She studied a class of ninth graders in the United States, using what she calls a 'thinking aloud approach' which consists of asking learners to perform a task and to verbalise their thought process as they do it. From her findings she drew up a list of strategies used by 'successful' and 'unsuccessful' readers in the class. This will be useful to consider as we think through the issue of what best to do in supporting adolescent readers. This is how Carol Horsenfeld described what her learners did when reading:

Successful readers tended to:
- keep the meaning of the passage in mind;
- read in broad phrases;
- skip inessential words;
- guess from context the meaning of unknown words;
- have a good self-concept as a reader.

Unsuccessful readers tended to:
- lose the meaning of sentences as soon as they decoded them;
- read word-by-word or in short phrases;
- rarely skip words;
- turn to the glossary for the meaning of new words;
- have a poor self concept as a reader.

Furthermore, her 'successful' readers tended to identify the grammatical category of words; demonstrate sensitivity to a different word order in the foreign language; examine illustrations; read the title and make inferences from it; use orthographical information; use the glossary as a last resort; look up words correctly; be persistent if unsuccessful at decoding a word or phrase; recognise cognates; evaluate their guesses.

After being given this list of strategies, one of her 'unsuccessful readers' commented: 'I just never thought of doing that'. A telling statement. Since this learner then practised some of the strategies and improved her reading, the research suggests that there is indeed value in laying bare the reading process for learners. It is interesting to note, however, that the learner who made the above comment did not learn to use all of the strategies of the 'successful' reader; she never did learn to identify the grammatical function of words, nor to skip inessential words. She nevertheless became a more efficient reader than she had been.

Horsenfeld (ibid) concludes that, though teachers often give learners support in pre-reading or post-reading activities, they rarely intervene when pupils are in the process of reading and that such intervention could be useful to learners. She suggests a possible support strategy:

> '... a teacher might:
> 1. assign the first paragraph of a story for silent reading;
> 2. ask several student volunteers to identify words which were new to them and to describe their strategies with these words;
> 3. discuss identified strategies with the entire class. The sequence – silent reading, disclosure and discussion – can be used with several paragraphs.'

More recent research (Macaro, 1998) on developing learner strategies, has developed the idea of 'strategy training'. The study, based at the University of Reading, involved four schools in which pupils in Year 8 and Year 10 were encouraged to use more strategies more often than they had previously done. The team of researchers devised a Strategy Training Booklet *to encourage the pupils to use more of a predefined set of strategies by getting them to record every time they used that strategy* and to encourage them *to develop their own strategies for learning – ones that they felt most comfortable with.* For instance, pupils were asked to record on one page of the booklet, over a period of four months, when they used a dictionary under the headings 'at home' or 'in class'! Other pages were explicit about the types of strategies which people could try out. An interesting result of the project, amongst many, was that boys found the experience of strategy training more beneficial than girls. Much work still needs to be done in this area of language teaching, but there is emerging a clear indication that it is possible to teach pupils to be better readers.

LISTENING TO THE TEXT

In Pathfinder 33, *Stimulating grammatical awareness*, Rendall argues that in order to develop accurate orthography from early on in the language learning process learners must be introduced to the sounds of words at the same time as their written equivalent. Also there is some evidence (Williams 1986) to suggest that listening to texts can help develop reading comprehension skills. Such listening might include tapes accompanying graded readers, texts recorded by the Foreign Language Assistant, the teacher reading to the class, older learners reading to younger learners, more confident readers reading to their less confident peers. However, the rate at which text is read aloud is much slower than normal reading speed, and though this strategy might help with comprehension, it is less beneficial in developing reading efficiency. The fluent reader reads quickly. Developing reading speed then may also be a strategy useful to discuss with learners.

DEVELOPING THE RATE AT WHICH LEARNERS READ

No one would suggests that as teachers of foreign languages we should spend too much of our limited class time on teaching speed reading, nevertheless this area of expertise could offer some useful pointers. *The Speed Reading Book* by Tony Buzan (1997) is a good example of such work and gives a clear idea of the type of advances which have been made in this area. It is a self-access course during which the reader undertakes a series of self-assessed reading exercises, noting the time it takes to accomplish each. This notion of beating your own record or establishing your 'personal best' time for reading a text of a certain length and complexity will be attractive to some learners. Skimming and scanning exercises could also help in developing the speed at which learners read. These might include exercises involving counting – how many times does the word '*Schule*' occur on page x?; exercises involving searching – look at page x – where does y live?; looking for themes – find words associated with food on page z. Whether or not you begin to introduce such activities into your everyday languages lessons, it will be important for learners to understand early on that it is not always profitable to read every word at a consistently slow speed and that an increase in speed can alleviate some of the frustration associated with reading for pleasure in a foreign language.

CiLT

3. Focus on the classroom

THE ROLE OF THE TEACHER

In some ways the measure of success in a programme of reading for pleasure is the extent to which the teacher is redundant. By this I mean that it is learners who need to choose what they read and who need to develop the self discipline to read, usually alone, in silence or near silence. Having said this, in order to create an appropriate learning environment the teacher will have prepared the ground well. Self discipline is important since there needs to be a sense of order for effective independent reading to take place. The teacher plays a central role in establishing good working practices and fostering the reading habit. The teacher needs to gauge the kinds of texts learners may be drawn to reading. Then there is the selection process during which he or she must seek out enough texts of an appropriate level both in terms of interest and maturity, but also of linguistic complexity. It is also important that reading strategies are taught alongside a programme of reading for pleasure. So the teacher's role as a facilitator, organiser, reference point and role model is non-interventionist which is often difficult where the norm is for the teacher to tightly control classroom procedures.

TEACHERS WORKING TOGETHER

Bo Lundahl from the University of Malmö in Sweden has worked closely with groups of teachers to establish reading programmes in local classrooms. He set up a training programme with teachers of pupils aged eleven to twelve during which they developed their ideas about fostering reading. Teachers discussed strategies and then, back at school, implemented them and gave learners opportunities to read English children's books. Bo interviewed both teachers and learners, inviting the latter to describe their attitude to books and to reading. The response was positive from the majority of learners – they focused on the opportunity to try something different, claiming that their capacity to learn was not fully recognised in the normal classroom.

He discovered that, by their own admission, all of the teachers involved in the programme had underestimated learners' ability to read. Although many of them were initially uncertain about how to use the books, they were pleasantly surprised at their pupils' enthusiasm and ability to cope.

Most significantly he discovered that the most successful ways of using books were found in those schools in the project where more than one teacher was involved, where teachers were able to instill confidence, where the teachers were able and allowed to create a relaxed learning environment and where teachers dared to make a shift in their approach away from the controlled language classroom. Teachers helped their pupils into the texts using shared reading techniques and pre-reading activities, reading leading to drama, reading leading to writing or to discussion.

Developing a reading programme need not and should not be the responsibility of a teacher working alone. Rather there needs to be a shift in the thinking of a whole department to see reading for pleasure as a valuable area to develop.

THE ROLE OF THE LEARNER

Much depends on learner attitudes for a programme of reading for pleasure to work efficiently. Perhaps by watching eye movements, we might be able to detect whether or not a learner is reading, but we cannot know what is actually going on in his or her head. It is up to the learner to take some responsibility. There are advantages for both teachers and learners once such an expectation is established, best expressed, I think, by Mark Clarke and Sandra Silberstein from the University of Michigan,

> 'First, it puts the teacher in their place, emphasising the individuality of students and reducing the compulsion we sometimes feel to control classroom activity. This relieves us of feelings of guilt and frustration occasioned by unsuccessful attempts at coercing the students to keep together. Second, it puts the responsibilty for learning squarely on the shoulders of the students, which is where it belongs.'

CLASS READERS – A SWEDISH APPROACH FOR LOW ATTAINERS

I have assumed so far that any programme of reading for pleasure will be based on learners choosing from a range of texts. This need not necessarily be the only approach to developing reading for pleasure. We might also consider the use of class readers. At one time this was popular in the UK but there has been a marked decline over the past twenty years. Since there is expertise in the effective use of class readers within English departments in the UK and in MFL departments internationally, it is an area which deserves revisiting.

The second phase of the Swedish project discussed above serves as a good example of the usefulness of developing approaches to class readers. To continue the story, the majority of pupils involved in the project were enthusiastic about their experiences reading English texts within a freer environment than they had generally been used to. However, there was a minority of learners whose reactions were much less positive. These were often low attaining pupils and reluctant learners. These learners concentrated on difficulties or problems they encountered in the reading project.

Because of this response Bo Lundahl, the leader of the project, began a reading project with Year 8 low attainers (thirteen- to fourteen-year-olds). This project had a different focus and lasted for one academic year. The profile of the group of learners was varied, but generally they were used to reading only short articles in English, they read very little in Swedish, their mother tongue, and were poorly motivated. He used a novel, *Stone Fox* by John Reynolds Gardiner (1980), and over the course of the year '*they journeyed into the text together*'. This journey consisted of many pre-reading and post-reading acivities which drew learners into the book, some of which are listed below. Lundahl's work may serve as a useful starting point for teachers interested in developing similar work with foreign language texts. What is interesting to note is his emphasis on using authentic text with low attainers – his focus on context and setting rather than lexical and grammatical items in the activities he sets.

   RESPONSE TO LITERATURE

Some worthwhile post-reading activities

1. Reading journal/reading log.
2. Let a student devise questions for the book. (*Why, what, where, who, how?*) The questions will be given to those reading the book next.
3. Similar approach as above but the questions should have no obvious answer. (*Do you think that . . .?*)
4. State (in writing) at least three reasons for reading the book – or against reading it.
5. Describe a character. The description should relate to the reader. (*Do you like the person? Why? Why not? Would you like to know him? Why? Why not? Would you like to be like him or her? Why? Why not?*)
6. Describe a picture in the book in as much detail as possible. (*What does it tell you? Does it show an important incident in the novel? In what way?*)
7. Make a family tree – use information about the main character and his or her family.
8. Draw a map of an area or an important place described in the book. Obviously, this works best if the novel is not illustrated already. The student can continue by explaining the drawing in writing – or to the teacher or to friends.
9. Write a short letter about one of the incidents to somebody in the book.
10. A character portrait in the form of a 'Wanted' or 'Missing' poster. To be displayed in the classroom!
11. Write a diary from the point of view of one of the characters. One day in the life of . . .
12. The film of the book. Design a poster for the 'film of the book'. Give the title, the stars playing specific characters (Clint Eastwood as … and starring Madonna as …).
13. The blurb of a book – provided the book does not already have a blurb (text about the contents on the back cover).
14. Read this book! Design an advertisement where you state reasons for buying it – or what the critics have had to say about it. Use your imagination! Ads are displayed on classroom walls.
15. A short extract reworked as a play. Perform in front of the class!
16. Interviewing the writer – a role play. Perform!
17. Would it make a movie? Write about it! Read it out to the class!
18. A puppet play. Retell a short extract from the story with puppets. Especially good with fairy tales or legends from mythology. The best thing is if there is a simple puppet theatre so that the students can hide behind it. Can they make their own puppets?
19. Is this book worth borrowing? Role play a conversation between a librarian and a student.
20. Working with words – a lot of different possibilities, for instance a semantic field.
21. As a last resort, a review.

Whether such activities should be conducted in the target language or in the mother tongue is debatable and will inevitably depend on the learners and the department or teacher developing the work. Certainly the text will be in the target language. It may be that in the UK, where learners are not immersed in the language they learn at school through daily doses of television, richer discussions would emerge if at least some of the work were produced in the mother tongue. This may be particularly true where low attaining or reluctant learners are studying a class reader. There will still be a great deal of satisfaction at the end of the process from having read a novel or a short story in a foreign language. A greater depth of knowledge may also have been developed if many of the issues are discussed in the mother tongue. Since work on a class reader is likely to form a part of a scheme of work rather than representing the totality of the MFL experience for learners, it could be argued that such lessons in English around a foreign language text represent a judicious and legitimate use of the mother tongue. However, many departments embarking upon such a project may well wish to develop much of the work in the target language. The important point here is not to choose one approach or another, but to identify strategies which engage the learner in reading the language.

During the study of *Stone Fox* learners kept a Reading Journal in which they compiled their thoughts and reactions to the different parts and aspects of the novel. This is the introduction to that journal, giving learners a clear indication of its purpose and their teacher's expectations:

Bilaga 6

A few words on writing a reading journal

When you read a book I would like you to stop now and again to write down your thoughts in your exercise books – in English or in Swedish – about what you read. You can for instance

- ask questions (*I wonder why …? Why does he or she …?*);
- express your thoughts and feelings about people and events (*This makes me think about when … , I like the way … , I don't like it when …*);
- write down memories (*This makes me remember when …*);
- make comparisons (*I have read about something like this in …, I saw a film where …*);
- guess what is going to happen next.

If you do, you will probably be surprised about the things you did not think you knew until you put pen to paper.

One more thing: I will be interested in reading your journal.

CiLT

Learners, over the course of the year, were also given activities which required them to reflect upon different aspects of the story. You will find three examples of such activities below:

Bilaga 7
STONE FOX

❏ Words to describe the book:

....

....

• Things I liked about the book:

....

....

❏ Things I didn't like:

....

....

• Something that surprised me was that

....

....

❏ My thoughts about the ending:

....

....

❏ Did you *think* it was going to end like this? Did you *want* it to end like this?

....

• How did you want it to end – if you wanted a different type of ending?

....

....

....

❏ The best part of the book is when

....

because ....

....

....

....

Bilaga 8

People in Sweden could have the same type of problems as Willy's grandfather. How would you solve the problem if you were in Willy's shoes? Try to think of as many solutions as possible (funny, mad or serious)!

Few examples of such work with longer foreign language texts exist in the UK at present, particularly for learners in their first three years of learning a language. There are many examples of techniques for drawing pupils into such texts in the teaching of English as a first language. It may be worthwhile discussing with English department colleagues the methods they use for developing reading skills with learners who find reading difficult. Certainly there have been developments in this area since the compulsory teaching, for instance, of Shakespeare was introduced into the curriculum at Key Stage 3. Here making the language accessible is an important aspect of the English teachers' work.

GUIDELINES FOR USING CLASS READERS

For those thinking of working on a class reader Christine Nuttall (1985) offers some useful guidelines. Though her book *Teaching reading skills in a foreign language* is now some years old, it still represents for me the most useful and readable practical guide for the establishment of reading for pleasure in the MFL curriculum. Her guidelines on the use of Class Readers include the following:

- choose a book which is likely to appeal to most of your learners;
- when considering reading level, pitch it lower rather than higher, if you cannot find a book at a low enough level, do not use this approach;
- think about splitting the book into sections, possibly issuing it a chapter at a time, like a magazine serial (though this may be difficult to organise);
- assign a lot of the reading to homework and use lesson time for discussion;
- use the reader over a limited period – say half a term – and share this information with your learners;

- have as your aim learners' understanding of the writer's main message without paying too much attention to details of language;
- occasionally concentrate on a particular short passage in the book – maybe a page long – for more detailed work in class;
- finish off with a final piece of work which helps learners see the book as a whole.

Having introduced the notion of using a class reader in order to present longer foreign language texts to learners, I do nevertheless advocate that the best method is through offering a range of texts for learners to choose from and to read at their own pace both in class time and at home. Such texts may be supported by activities or not; learners' work on them may be assessed or not. This will depend on the needs of the learners and the teachers implementing the reading programme. What is important is that the work is well organised and systematic so that progression and continuity can be achieved term on term, year on year. There are some examples of such a systematic approach being developed in the UK context and these are described on the following pages.

SOME EXAMPLES OF PRACTICE FROM UK SCHOOLS

Over the past ten years some MFL departments in the UK have devised reading programmes. These tend to have similar broad aims which include:

- motivating learners to develop a reading habit;
- helping learners develop their language proficiency through reading in the target language;
- diminishing the fear that learners often experience when faced with unfamiliar texts;
- exploring the medium country's culture through books and magazines.

I have included six examples here from teachers and schools where reading for pleasure is seen as an important element in the development of learners' reading skills. I present the examples through documentation provided by the schools.

Stoke Newington School had just begun setting up a reading scheme as this Pathfinder went to press. The department ran a pilot project in the Summer term prior to launching a programme of reading for pleasure for Year 8 and 9 pupils. We have reproduced below the original aims of the project, the problems encountered and the future plans for the implementation of the programme. We also include the evaluative questionnaire given to pupils which the department used to inform the full implementation of the programme.

Stoke Newington School

---

1 THE STOKE NEWINGTON SCHOOL PROJECT

PILOT READING PROJECT – STOKE NEWINGTON SCHOOL

WHY?
Although we had reading materials in our department, their use was haphazard depending on each teacher's interest. Encouraged by a successful bid for literacy funding, extra reading materials were bought and a pilot scheme focusing on Year 8 was put into action in the last half of the summer term.

Our aim in undertaking the pilot was to test out recently acquired reading materials and students' responses to lessons dedicated specifically to 'reading for pleasure'.

HOW?
The reading pilot took place once every two weeks, involving two Year 8 classes, one French and the other Spanish. In an effort to emphasise the importance of reading in the foreign language and the benefits derived from it, the lessons were timetabled in the Resource Centre (Library). Each student was given a Record Card where they recorded what they read and their responses to it. They had free choice of what they wanted to read and were encouraged to read quietly in pairs or by themselves.

EVALUATION
In evaluating the relative success or otherwise of the reading pilot, the students' opinions were sought along with those of the language teachers involved and the Resource Centre Co-ordinator.

Students' responses to the questionnaire were surprisingly detailed and not always limited to one word responses. Asked what they enjoyed the most, answers varied from, *'it's quiet'* and *'you don't have to write much'* to *'I enjoyed the fact that all you had to do is read. No questions were asked so you could do it at your own pace'* and the inevitable *'nothing'!*

Responses to questions relating to what they enjoyed the least, and whether there was sufficient choice of resources, highlighted students' criticisms of the way they were asked to work, whether individually or in pairs and the level of difficulty and sufficient range of materials.

Students tended to believe that they had learnt something from the experience whether it be *'some new words'* or *'not to bother about understanding every single word'*.

WHAT NEXT?

Taking into account all the positive and pertinent opinions expressed by students and teachers alike, it was felt worthwhile continuing the reading lessons on a bigger scale in the new academic year. Consequently:

- reading lessons have been requested by our department to be timetabled in the Resource Centre once every two weeks for Year 8 and 9 Spanish and French classes;
- with advice from the Resource Centre Co-ordinator, and building on the experience of the English department, we hope to provide 'tips and strategies' for reading in the modern foreign language and more structured opportunities for individual reading, pair-work and group-work;
- we aim to work alongside the Resource Centre Co-ordinator when choosing books from the local lending library service and, when possible, buy further resources including CD-ROMs;
- existing resources are to be organised so that the level of difficulty of the books is clear. Also in an attempt to exploit the Mary Glasgow magazines more effectively, the different articles are to be divided into separate folders on 'sports', 'cartoons', 'activities', 'culture', etc. We hope this will highlight more clearly what is on offer and discourage endless flicking through magazines from beginning to end in two minutes.

Reading in the Resource Centre will be evaluated more thoroughly at the end of the forthcoming academic year to continue trying to improve the students' experience of 'reading for pleasure'.

Evaluation of Reading Lessons in the Resource Centre

1. What did you enjoy most about reading in the Resource Centre?

....

....

2. What did you enjoy least about reading in the Resource Centre?

....

....

3. Was there enough choice of what to read?   Yes ☐   No ☐

4. If you answered 'NO', what else would you have liked included?

....

5. Have you found the material: easy to read ☐   not too bad ☐   difficult ☐

6. Do you feel more confident about using the dictionary now?   Yes ☐   No ☐

7. What do you think you have learnt from reading in French/Spanish?

....

....

8. Do you prefer reading: individually ☐   in pairs ☐   as a group ☐

9. Do you have any suggestions to improve reading in the Resource Centre?

....

Record de Lectura

Nombre:.............................   Clase: ....

Titulo	Fecha	Fantastico	Interesante	Aburrido	Facil/Dificil

CiLT

Patchway School in Bristol has an established programme of reading for pleasure. Below we have reproduced the reading policy of the department together with examples of learner reading diaries for French and German. Reading periods take place in the Library. We have included the Library timetable to demonstrate how rotational arrangements can be put in place. Many of the reading resources are duplicated and stored in classrooms so that learners do not have to wait until the reading period if they wish to continue reading in between times.

PATCHWAY
HIGH SCHOOL

2 PATCHWAY SCHOOL, BRISTOL — READING POLICY

RATIONALE
Reading is an essential part of foreign language learning. It encourages independent learning, extends vocabulary, reinforces structures and brings enjoyment.

PURPOSES
We aim to train pupils to develop their reading skills for the following purposes:
1. to deduce meaning;
2. to identify and extract information;
3. to summarise texts and read for gist;
4. to develop reference skills;
5. to increase vocabulary and range of structures;
6. to see reading as an intrinsically enjoyable experience;
7. to link with other language skills.

GUIDELINES
1. Appropriate materials must be provided – to include factual and non-factual texts, texts with pictures, signs, authentic texts, cartoons, comics, stories/texts by other pupils, poems, rhymes, magazines, books, etc.
2. Reading opportunities for Year 7 will be mainly in text book.
3. Graded reading schemes will be in use for Years 8–9. They will complete a reading diary.
4. Library facilities will be used as appropriate.
5. Teachers will teach dictionary/reference skills using agreed resources.
6. Tape-recordings of some stories/texts will be available.
7. Materials appropriate to GCSE and A level will be used with Years 10 and 11 and the sixth form – reading for enjoyment included.
8. Reading material will also be on display in rooms etc.

CONCLUSION
Good practice in reading will aid learning and progression.

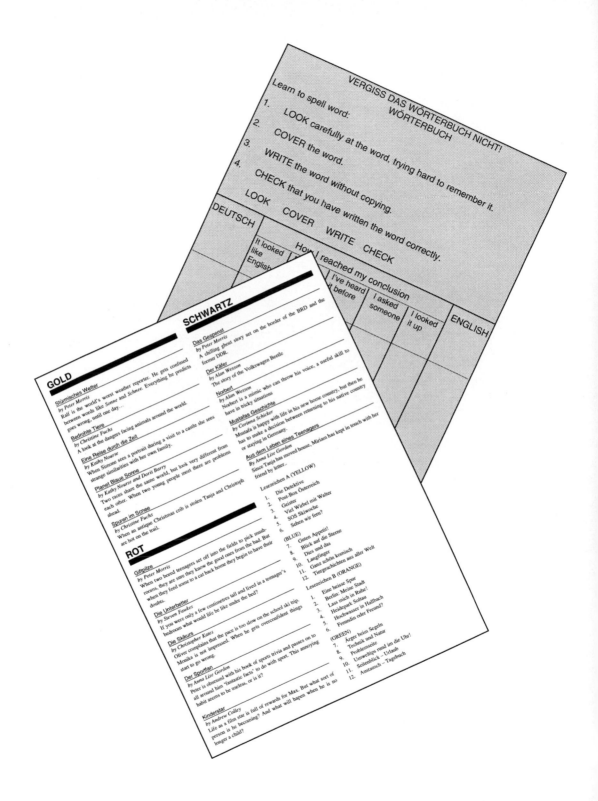

CILT

LIBRARY TIMETABLE
AUTUMN TERM

WEEK 1			WEEK2		
Monday, 22 Sept	P.3	8Ge3 RP	Thursday, 20 Nov	P.5	8GE4 GC
	P.4	8Ge1 BG		P.6	8Fr3 GC
Wednesday, 24 Sept	P.5	9Fr4 EC	Friday, 21 Nov	P.5	9Fr1 KW
	P.6	9Fr3 EC		P.6	9Ge3 GC

WEEK 1			WEEK1		
Monday, 6 Oct	P.3	8Fr3 GC	Monday, 24 Nov	P.3	8Ge2 JM
	P.4	8Fr2 KW		P.4	8Fr1 RP
Wednesday, 8 Oct	P.5	9Ge3 GC	Wednesday, 26 Nov	P.5	9Fr6 LS
	P.6	9Fr1 KW		P.6	9Fr2 LS

WEEK 2			WEEK2		
Thursday, 16 Oct	P.5	8Ge4 GC	Thursday, 4 Dec	P.5	8Ge1 BG
	P.6	8Fr4 EC		P.6	8Ge3 RP
Friday, 17 Oct	P.5	9Fr2 LS	Friday, 5 Dec	P.5	9Fr3 EC
	P.6	9Fr6 LS		P.6	9Fr5 KW

WEEK 1			WEEK1		
Monday, 20 Oct	P.3	8Ge2 JM	Monday, 8 Dec	P.3	8Fr4 EC
	P.4	8Fr1 RP		P.4	8Fr2 KW
Wednesday, 22 Oct	P.5	9Ge2 JM	Wednseday, 10 Dec	P.5	9Ge2 JM
	P.6	9Ge1 JM		P.6	9Ge1 JM

WEEK 2			WEEK2		
Thursday, 6 Nov	P.5	8Ge1 BG	Thursday, 18 Dec	P.5	8GE4 GC
	P.6	8Ge3 RP		P.6	8Fr3 GC
Friday, 7 Nov	P.5	9Fr3 EC			
	P.6	9Fr5 KW			

The MFL department at Cotham Grammar School in Bristol has successfully linked their pupils' reading with creative writing. Here learners write story books for younger readers in the school. This is a description of the scheme written by the head of department.

3 COTHAM GRAMMAR SCHOOL, BRISTOL

READING FOR PLEASURE

BACKGROUND
We had a few class readers which were gradually growing old, and no money to replace them. A little lateral thinking produced the idea that we could simply make our own. This was usually done as a creative writing block, and linked to end-of-topic goals, so that creation of a reader might constitute the written assessment for that unit. Explaining it in French/German/Spanish to the class or, more usually, to the teacher, might well become oral assessment. The readers then were placed in the faculty library and were available for classes to read or for individuals to choose.

TOPICS
Readers were made by students of all ages from Years 7 to 13. Below are some typical topics and treatments.

Many students used ICT in their work, but handwritten work proved equally interesting to the readers.

In all cases, a high level of illustration based on actual sentences in the text was encouraged and all were told: *'You are writing for younger children – make sure they will understand.'*

We have begun the same process this year, with the addition that any good display done by a whole class, when removed from the wall, is then bound together in book form, because I have found that students are quite willing to look through 30 versions of the same basic idea! For example, this year, at the beginning of Year 7, we ran a competition after approximately one month's work to produce a display poster entitled, *'C'est moi'* or *'Das bin ich'*. Obviously this produced quite a lot of variety and included some personal photographs and amusing drawings. We now have two A4-sized books for our library.

Topic	Interpretation	Comment
1. School Year 8	*Le Monstre du Collège*	Students invented a monster who lived in school – opportunity to describe him, what he did, where he lived, what he ate and drank, etc. Tone: humorous Oral interpretation: simulated radio programme, in which people were interviewed about the monster in THEIR school
2. Personal details Year 7	My autobiography – collection of personal information and puzzles, exercises and games based on the topic area	These were built up during the first school year. Students added information, photos, etc when time allowed. They invented puzzles and games
3. Food and drink Year 8/9	*Zu Hause allein* – a week spent at home with parents away – organise menu for self and, on one evening, for a friend as well	The week's menu, shopping list. Dinner arrangements for evening when friend invited. Finished with account of what they had done
4. Travel at home and abroad Year 10	Transcript of a radio programme	Dialogue of planning itinerary, discussing possibilities, likely difficulties, etc
Year 8	Children's story based on modes of transport	Titles like '*Le Petit Autobus rouge*'
5. The year 3000 Year 11	Personal profiles; News reports and articles; Recipes; Travel articles; Imaginative stories, etc	A huge variety. Many humorous and interesting ideas
6. The environment – protection of the forest Year 12	Write a children's story with a moral theme linked to the topic area – a teaching tool!	Beautiful children's books with picture and small amount of text of good quality per page were produced. This was an early Year 12 activity
7. My home town Year 9	Brochures at many levels	Simple: *on peut . . .* *il y a . . .* Full descriptions and opinions. Puzzles – can you recognise it? Ideal itinerary (guide book)
8. On exchange Year 8/9	Series of postcards home Diary (past tense); Collection of 'realia' with own notes	Chance to use a wide variety of language, and cover a number of tenses and topic areas
9. Holidays abroad Year 10/11	Letter to penfriend on return; Story based in the country chosen	Students generally used travel brochure as a stimulus and researched the area with teacher's help

We are now quite heavily involved in written coursework at GCSE. Having seen some of the beautiful work produced by Year 10 students, I can see a real future source of books once the work is no longer required by the examiners – it may also give some students an idea of what is required of them when producing coursework.

ACCURACY

This is a thorny question. Students go through quite a lot of refining of their work before producing the final version, but some errors do remain. I find I have to let these stand, unless they are of a very serious nature. Before releasing the book, after assessment, we try to do some corrections.

WHEN DO WE READ?

At the moment, this is a somewhat haphazard activity. We are currently writing schemes of work in which reading blocks appear, and will book classes into the library on a regular basis so that some of the reading takes place in an environment conducive to quiet reading. This will draw students' attention to the books placed in the library and perhaps encourage them to read in a foreign language outside of class hours.

RECORDING OUR EFFORTS

A simple sheet, recording date and title and opinions in tick box form for younger students. At KS4 and 5, to include also a space to write a short synopsis and opinion with reason.

SAVING MONEY

As money continues to be a problem and we are unlikely to be able to afford any commercially produced reading schemes at the moment, I am continuing to look for ways of updating our store of reading matter. I have had some ideas:

1. Extract all the 'Reading' photocopiable sheets from the teacher's resource files we possess, copy on to brightly coloured strong card, possibly different colours for different levels of activity, sort into collections, possibly topics or levels of difficulty.

2. We are collecting colourful catalogues and have already large quantities of authentic material brought over from France in particular. Some of these pieces would lend themselves quite readily to being made into reading cards.

Vincent Everett, a teacher from Fakenham High School and College, uses information cards collected from magazines to motivate learners to read. Each type of card (for example *fiche football*, *fiche musique*, *fiche cuisine*) is kept in a reading resource box which is part of the classroom library. Learners choose the card they wish to work from during the reading period. Their reading is guided by a worksheet such as that reproduced. Learners are taught to be explicit about the reading strategies they are using so that, when they progress to more independent reading in MFL, they read more successfully. Work on the reading cards, which is very structured, runs alongside reading periods in the school library where there is a selection of MFL texts for them to choose from. Occasionally Vincent suggests that a learner works through his 'How to read in any language' worksheets (see p 10) which again attempt to make explicit to learners the reading strategies which they employ.

4 FAKENHAM HIGH SCHOOL AND COLLEGE

FABRIZIO RAVANELLI

Nationalité: italienne
Né le 11 décembre 1968 à Pérouse (Italie)
Taille: 1,88 m - **Poids:** 80 kg
Poste: attaquant
Clubs successifs: Pérouse, Avellino, Casartena, Reggiana, Juventus (Ita), Middlesbrough (Ang), Olympique Marseille (Fra)
Palmarès: champion d'Italie et vainqueur de la Coupe d'Italie en 1995, vainqueur de la Coupe de l'UEFA en 1993 et de la Champions League en 1996 (Juventus)
Sélections: 20 (8 buts)

Fils cadet d'un modeste employé de l'ENEL (l'EDF italienne) et d'une ouvrière du textile, Fabrizio Ravanelli caresse ses premiers ballons sur le terrain pelé de l'Oratoire de Mugnano, un village des environs de Pérouse. Là-bas, les anciens se souviennent avec fierté du gamin costaud et turbulent. Il a 14 ans et déjà les cheveux gris: «Tout jeune, je faisais déjà vieux!», rigole Fabrizio. Mais tout jeune, il fait aussi fureur balle au pied. Attaquant puissant et efficace, il fait son apprentissage à Pérouse (90 matches, 41 buts), Avellino (7 matches et une incompatibilité d'humeur avec ses dirigeants), la Casertana (27 matches, 12 buts) et la Reggiana (66 matches, 24 buts), avant de signer dans le club de ses rêves (il en est un super *tifoso* depuis l'enfance): la Juventus. Il y réalise le doublé (1995), remporte la C3 (1993) et la Champions League (1996, c'est lui qui marque le but de la Juve en finale) mais se voit bientôt poussé vers la sortie. Après une triste parenthèse à Middlesbrough, «Plume blanche» retrouve le sourire à l'OM, où il débarque fin 1997. Privé de Mondial pour cause de broncho-pneumonie, il espère désormais offrir un titre majeur à des supporters qui l'adorent.

OCTOBRE 1998

Note: *Onze Mondial* is published each month (ISSN: 0995-6921) and costs 259FF for an annual subscription. In October 1998 they were still publishing eight football cards in each issue, and advertising cards 45-116 which could be obtained from VPC Onze Mondial BP 4-59718 Lille Cedex 9 France (tel: 03 20 12 12 12)

Guided Reading Strategies for *Onze Mondial* Football Cards

This sheet will help you to read any of the cards in the series, to maximise your understanding and to improve your confidence and skill in reading real French!

Answer any questions in **bold** type on another sheet of paper.

1. Look at the picture and the player's name. Do you know this player? Can you tell his nationality from his name? Can you identify his club from his shirt? **Write down as much as you know about this player, his life, his career, his clubs.**

2. Now turn over and look at the basic information given at the top of the page. **Can you guess what is meant by each of these categories:**

Nationalité	*Né le*	*Taille*	*Poids*	*Poste*
Clubs Successifs	*Palmarès*	*Sélections*		

    (Hint: looking at the information will help you work out what each section means.)

3. **What position does your player prefer?**

Goalkeeper	Central defender	Midfield	Forward	Sweeper

4. **Write all the information you have understood about your player from this section.**

5. Now look at the longer piece of writing about your player. **Find, and note down, all the people, places, clubs and stadiums that are mentioned.**

6. **Now find all the dates and numbers** (in figures or in words).

7. Here are some words that are likely to appear in writing about football. Can you find the French for them on your card? If you are not sure, look them up in your dictionary. Are there any other words you think you will need to recognise? **Look them up and write down what you find.**

Season	Goal	Shirt	Career	Club
To Sign	Trophy	Pitch	Match	First Half	Transfer List

8. **What is the general picture you can make out of your player's career? Are there any particular incidents or events you think you understand?**

9. **See if you can find the following information on these individual players:**

    *   Which English club did *Skoblar* coach?
    *   How many goals did *Sibierski* get in one match?
    *   Why did *Ince* go from West Ham to Manchester?
    *   What did *Ravelli's* parents do?
    *   Who is *Passi's* brother?
    *   What does '*Cuca*' mean?
    *   What was *Amunike's* role in Nigeria's 1994 African championship?

This description of a reading scheme was provided by the head of department of a comprehensive school in Essex which linked into the whole school reading policy. Dedicated time for reading for pleasure was provided within the PSE programme of the school. The MFL reading programme fitted into this context.

ESSEX COMPREHENSIVE SCHOOL

READING FOR PLEASURE IN MFL – A MEANS TO AN END

An example of a reading scheme set up in an 11–16 Comprehensive school in Essex (mixed ability in KS3, some in-class support for SEN, De/Fr equal FL1)

THE BACKGROUND

The school had in place a Reading Policy devised by the English Department where pupils used a five-star rating system to record and comment on books they read in their free time or in the time devoted to reading in the Pastoral programme.

SETTING UP THE SCHEME

- Responsibility for setting up the scheme was given to two native speakers of the department, one French one German.
- Authentic texts (real books) were purchased in Germany and France with funds from the department capitation allowance.
- Texts were read on to cassette (one book per cassette) by Foreign Language Assistants, as part of their assigned twelve hours, and native-speaker teachers.
- Tasks were devised in French and German taking into account a number of factors:

  - differentiation by task/outcome/pupil interest/pupil ability;
  - equality with regard to diversification of FL1;
  - cross curricular/whole school implication (see above);
  - involvement of pupils/development of independent learning;
  - teamwork/involvement of FLA/CPD implications;
  - motivation of reading a whole book of own choice.

THE SCHEME IN ACTION

- At the start of Year 8 pupils were issued with a reading record card (*Carte de Lecture/Lesekarte*); see examples. (The programme was initially designed for KS3.) Pupils were already used to having a personal cassette tape for speaking practice.
- Time was set aside for reading (and listening) during scheduled lesson time as part of a small group activity, at lunchtime/after-school sessions or as homework. Encouragement was given to the idea of MFL reading in the whole school reading time (see above).

- Materials were held 'centrally', i.e. one classroom location per language, tapes and books together with a 'catalogue' and a pupil signing out book. Books were small (usually paperback) – demands on storage space were minimal.
- Pupils were responsible for keeping their record card up to date for teacher inspection.
- Planning for the future involved integrating the MFL reading scheme into the school library database and loan system.

CiLT

Carte de Lecture

Nom: ....

Classe:..

J'ai commencé	J'ai fini	Titre	Auteur	Nombre d'étoiles	Commentaire	Activité numéro

Nombre d'étoiles

*****	C'était super
****	C'était bien
***	C'était pas mal
**	C'était pas bien
*	C'était horrible

Vocabulaire pour ton commentaire

très	very
intéressant	interesting
passionnant	exciting
drôle	funny
triste	sad
facile	easy
difficile	difficult
fatigant	boring

Activités

(Choisis les deux activités que tu préfères)

1. Copie et illustre dix mots nouveaux sur la liste. Enregistre les dix sur ta cassette.
2. Lis un passage sur ta cassette.
3. Fais une liste des personnages du livre.
4. Fais une couverture différente pour le livre.
5. Trouve un titre différent.
6. Fais une bande dessinée basée sur le livre.
7. Ecris l'histoire simplifiée pour un petit garçon/une petite fille.
8. Lis ton histoire sur la cassette.
9. Identifie des mots nouveaux dans le livre et écris les mots en français et en anglais.
10. Identifie des mots nouveaux et écris une phrase avec chaque mot.

Lesekarte

Name: ....

Klasse: ....

Wann begonnen?	Wann beendet?	Titel	Autor	Sternnummer	Kommentar	Aufgaben Nummer

Sternnummer

*****	Es war prima
****	Es war gut
***	Es war in Ordnung
**	Nicht so gut
*	Ich fand es furchtbar

Vokabelhilfe für deinen Kommentar

interessant	interesting
spannend	exciting
schwer	difficult
leicht	easy
lustig	funny
traurig	sad
langweillig	boring
ziemlich	rather
zu	too
sehr	very

Aufgaben

(zwei Aufgaben pro Buch bitte)
1. Zehn Vokabeln von der Karte kopieren und illustrieren und auf Kassette sprechen.
2. Eine Passage auf Kassette lesen.
3. Eine Liste der Charaktere schreiben.
4. Einen alternativen Buchdeckel designen.
5. Einen alternativen Titel finden.
6. Einen Cartoonstreifen designen.
7. Eine simple Version für Babys schreiben.
8. Das Buch auf Kassette lesen.
9. Extra Vokabeln im Buch identifizieren und in Deutsch und Englisch schreiben.
10. Neue Vokabeln im Buch identifizieren und einen Satz pro Vokabel schreiben.

CiLT

Gordano School, Bristol has systematically introduced reading for pleasure to younger learners for some years. Recently this work has paid dividends in the work of Year 10 pupils submitting coursework for their GCSE examinations. Similarly coursework focusing on reading and research has been produced by Year 12 and 13 pupils using texts which they have found on the Internet. This is a description of the recent developments in reading for pleasure at the school produced by the MFL department.

6 GORDANO SCHOOL, BRISTOL

READING FOR PLEASURE

A few years ago our reading scheme consisted of a number of boxes of ageing French and German readers, which were timetabled for use with our Year 8 and 9 groups. Many readers were in a dilapidated condition and had become a target for students who preferred to pass their time during reading lessons relentlessly adding pornographic details to the illustrations and obscene word balloons to the dialogues. If our aim was for students to be reading French and German for pleasure, then some students, perhaps a relatively small number, were taking no pleasure in doing so, and those who did take pleasure in reading in a foreign language were being presented with books that had been defaced.

Why? Well, we never actually caught anyone defacing a reader and so never had the opportunity to ask them why they were doing it, however we felt the scheme was failing for a number of reasons:

- we had never actually read the readers ourselves and thus had never spent any time considering how appropriate each reader was in terms of the interests, maturity, and reading skills of our target audiences;
- no outcomes were expected. The students were simply being asked to read quietly and that was all;
- the readers were sometimes being used inappropriately by us outside the timetabled slots, for a quiet lesson with a difficult group, or as an easy option when a cover lesson needed to be set.

So the dilapidated and defaced readers went in the bin, we had a good look at Pathfinder 2, *Reading for Pleasure in a Foreign Language*, bid for some curriculum development money and started again from scratch. One member of the department volunteered to relaunch the scheme and set about ordering inspection copies of every reader on the market and producing reading diaries. This was the plan:

- we would examine the readers carefully for interest level, maturity and readability and would buy only those which could be matched on all three counts to the needs of particular classes. Additionally, we would laminate individual pages from Mary Glasgow magazines to create a set of reading cards for our Year 7 classes;
- we would expect outcomes in terms of recording new vocabulary and, in the completion of reading diaries based on the model in the Pathfinder, or if the budget would not stretch to reading diaries, in the writing up in exercise books of a short critique of each reader using a comment bank on the board;
- we would use the readers more appropriately, adhering to the schedule and would not use them for an impromptu quiet lesson at the end of a hard day or as cover materials.

In the meantime a cut in our contact time for Years 8 and 9 has lead to reading lessons being scheduled half-termly, rather than fortnightly as planned. The drying up of curriculum development funding has meant that, although one member of the department has spent many, many hours designing a diary, we have printed only a limited number … BUT our KS3 students are now reading books which seem to appeal to them to a greater degree than before, they record vocabulary and write critiques and, significantly, the new readers have remained graffiti and obscenity free.

It has been difficult to find many readers written specifically for KS4, but some of the more demanding KS3 readers we have bought have appealed to our KS4 students, and more able students have been pushed to begin to summarise their readers and comment on them in greater depth by augmenting the phrases from our KS3 reading diaries with language lifted or adapted from authentic book and film reviews in text books.* (Below are two examples, 'Planet Blaue Sonne' is an early example, 'Stürmisches Wetter' was submitted as a piece of coursework.)

We are now beginning to look at the Internet as a source of reading material particularly for up-to-date material for sixth formers. Students need careful supervision and direction when surfing the Internet to ensure that they access appropriate material and to evaluate whether what they have found is useful. That said, our Year 13 students have been able to write their recent coursework on environmental issues using almost exclusively sources from the Internet. As a result they have been able to include in their work information, statistics, and quotes from press releases from Government bodies and pressure groups which they know are up to date and in some cases had been published only days before they began writing their coursework.

* For German, an example of a review can be found on p. 62 of *Lernpunkt Deutsch 2*. Models for writing critiques can be found on p. 28 of *Lernpunkt Deutsch 3*.

Planet Blaue Sonne

Die Geschichte heißt *Planet Blaue Sonne*. Der Titelheld und die
Titelheldin heißen Clauda und Thors. Die Geschichte spielt in der
Zukunft auf dem Planeten Blaue Sonne in zwei Städten, Zorit und
Waschik. Es handelt sich von zwei Völkern, die einander hassen, weil
Sie verschiedene Augenfarben haben.
   Ich habe die Geschichte interessant gefunden. Die Handlung ist sehr
ungewöhnlich. Mir haben die Illustrationen gefallen, sie sind hübsch
und bunt. Ich würde das Buch empfehlen.

By Grace Warrick

Stürmisches Wetter

Ich habe *Stürmisches Wetter* gelesen. Die Geschichte spielt in Deutschland. Der Titelheld ist
Ralf Meineke. Er hat ein Problem. Ralf ist Meterologe, obwohl die Kameras ihn nervös
machen. Wann Ralf nervös ist, verwechselt wie 'Sonne' und 'Schnee'. Sein Chef ist nicht
glücklich. Im Juni an einem schön Wochenende, gab es Staus nach Österrich auf der
Autobahn. Skier war in das Autos und Ralf war Schuld.

Ralf war sehr deprimiert, weil er wahrscheinlich auch arbeitslos war. Seine Frau, Katya, ein
gute Idee gehabt. Ralf und Katya können in Urlaub fahren. Ralf habe zwei Karten nach
Sibirien gekauft. Sibirien hat kein Sonne! Katya war nicht zufrieden. Ralf in die Stadt
gegangen, aber das Reisebüro war geschlossen. Ralf war nicht zufrieden. Ralf nach Hause
gefahren, aber sein Chef angerufen hat . . .

Ich habe die Geschichte sehr komisch gefunden. Mir hat die Illustrationen gefallen, weil Ralf
sehr gutaussehend ist! Ich würde das Buch empfehlen, weil es sehr erfreulich ist.

Jenni Orme

---

4.   Focus management issues

WHICH TEXTS?

There are two main positions taken in the debate about reading – two general approaches which appear to contradict each other. On the one hand there are those who look on texts as language practice tools. They take a skills-based approach to language teaching and learning. Here the language is built up bit by bit and there is a view of progression in the order and way in which language forms are introduced. Any reading must fit into a programme designed to produce such progression.

On the other hand there are those who see reading as an interactive process where the emphasis shifts from teaching to learning – from transmission of knowledge to interpretation of meaning. Knowledge of the language system becomes subordinated to content, in much the same way as is argued by Little, Devitt and Singleton (1989), mentioned earlier, who advocate the use of authentic texts. The place of graded readers in this approach is questionable since they do not offer the same opportunites for pupils to be involved in interpreting text and coming to their own understandng of the text. Research suggests that the substitution in a text of simpler words does not necessarily simplify the task of reading nor does, for example, sentence length have any measurable effect as far as simplification is concerned. So the whole area of graded readers is complex, though they make up a large proportion of the publications available for reading for pleasure, certainly in the UK.

What is clear from looking at a selection of reading resources now available is that there are resources on the market which cater for these different positions – there are topic-based reading cards, there are graded readers, there are simplified texts, books and CD-ROMs. These different reading resources have different purposes as far as learning is concerned and the distinction needs to be clear. Whilst language practice materials are an important part of MFL department resources, they do not provide a rich reading diet in themselves and will not help in developing a reading habit nor foster an interest in foreign language books if they are the only reading resources available.

Recently a group of MFL teachers was asked by the Qualifications and Curriculum Authority (QCA) to review a selection of publications designed for reading for pleasure. The initial findings of the teachers suggested that readers preferred texts which:

• are short, complete and journalistic in flavour;
• relate to their own experience of life;

- relate to their own popular culture;
- are immediately attractive;
- are totally up to date.

But should relevance to learners' lives drive the curriculum? Such a response would be shortsighted, I think. To succumb to the seduction of providing pupils with what is perceived as 'relevant' reading is to go down the path of impoverishment, to the 'retreat from text' which English colleagues described in the 1980s. Pupils find reading difficult, so give them less to read. Result? They don't and can't read.

Teachers have often commented that pupils do not so much read as browse. Given the need to find appealing texts for this generation of browsers, then, resources need to be chosen judiciously. There is a wide range of materials available, all of which could form part of a library. Many different sorts of texts can draw pupils into reading. They include simplified texts designed for language learners, abridged stories, parallel texts, children's books, translations, familiar stories, magazines, newspapers in accessible format, strip cartoons, joke books, books with a practical intent, books designed for browsing, texts from the Internet, reading schemes which include fiction and non-fiction, magazines to accompany video and public information designed for young readers. On a local level it is important to gauge, by questionnaire or other means, what your learners read, if they read, and if not, what they are interested in and what might draw them into reading.

WHERE TO FIND TEXTS

It cannot be denied that establishing a programme of reading for pleasure requires considerable financial investment. The first port of call in your search for such resources will be publishers. A list of addresses is included in Appendix 2 at the back of this book. Resources for reading for pleasure have improved in recent years, with most major educational publishers producing some form of either reading scheme or books to fit into such a scheme. It will also be useful to investigate publishers from the target country. A good starting point could be European Schoolbooks or the European Bookshop, addresses for which can be found with the list of publishers.

Link schools may also prove a rich resource. Alison Taylor in Pathfinder 9, *Languages Home and Away,* describes activities to be done in the library during the school visit abroad. She suggests useful books and magazines together with the organisation of a book and resources exchange.

More ideas for maximising the benefits of visits abroad

Organise a books/games/cassettes swap. Foreign colleagues can ask for unwanted books from their classes. An announcement in the staffroom is also an excellent way of obtaining more materials. In order to get the right sort of books it is useful to make suggestions. The following list may be helpful:

French books
J'aime lire
Folio Junior
Folio Benjamin
Lutin poche de l'école de loisirs
Collection rose
Collection verte
Je bouquine: Bayard Presse Jeune

Magazines
Pomme d'Api
Okapi
Astrapi
Pif Gadget
Oncle Picsou
Jacinthe
20 ans
OK
Onze
Nous deux (and other *romans-photos*)
Ça m'intéresse
Science et Vie

Sometimes books with cassettes are donated, which is an added bonus. If your school is travelling by coach, transporting the books is easy. It is also possible to send them from a French railway station as a *paquet à petite vitesse.* This takes about two weeks to arrive and is relatively cheap in view of the weight.

German magazines
Trend
Die Staffette

Books
DTV Pocket lesen-nachdenken-mitreden
Ravensburger Taschenbücher – Jeans Reihe
Die drei Fragezeichen
Karl May series

Spanish magazines
Chica
Cambio 16
Blanco y Negro
Tiempo
El País Semanal
Muy interesante
Quercus (ecología)
Tribu

Cartoon strips
Zipe y Zape
Mortadelo y Filemón
TBO

Italian magazines
Topolino
Paperino
Monello
Tex
Candy Candy
Amica
Anna

Newspapers
ABC
Diario 16
El País
Vanguardia

From *Languages Home and Away*, Pathfinder 9

You may also find the CILT Resource Library in London or one of the regional Comenius Centres a useful reference point for such resources. You will find the addresses for all of these in Appendix 3 at the back of this publication. A visit is advisable, but the co-ordinator will be able to discuss with you over the phone the resources which are available. This will give you the opportunity to look at resources before you buy.

You may also wish to spend time in bookshops of the target country. This can be a very interesting experience, though you will need time to select suitable titles. It is advisable to do this selection with a colleague if possible since the linguistic level of publications is sometimes difficult to gauge. You may also find it useful to discuss with teachers from the target country publications which are designed for adolescent readers from that country with a low reading age.

BUILDING A RESOURCE BOX FROM THE INTERNET

The Internet is a good source of reading material if used selectively. In his recent publication in the InfoTech series, *WWW/The Internet* (CILT 1998), Terry Atkinson offers guidance on conducting searches and building resource banks for use in the classroom. His section on reading for pleasure will be of use to anyone building a bank of resources from the Net. It is reproduced here to give a taste of the ideas Atkinson has developed. I highly recommend a closer look at the book.

SOME SUGGESTED ACTIVITIES

A reading file
Reading for pleasure can play a valuable part in language learning and offers scope for differentiation, extension, choice and flexibility. The Internet offers a wide choice of reading matter that can be printed out and used to form a classified reading scheme.

Using a colour printer (cost around £200), high quality printouts of Internet pages can be made on a wide variety of topics of interest for children in a particular year group, e.g. hobbies, pets, school, sport, pop music, fashion, home pages of young people, environmental issues, news reports, places of interest.

The printouts can then be classified according to degree of difficulty of the language. Three categories might be used and for this it is important to obtain a range of materials within each category. A system of colour coding can be used to indicate the level of each printout. The printouts can be stored in loose-leaf folders, protected in plastic envelopes and made available to be used in lessons in various ways:

- as a filler for pupils who have finished early;
- as an optional activity in some lessons;
- as part of a carousel of activities.

The collection of printouts is ongoing and a number of folders can be accumulated so that these folders can be rotated between teachers to ensure that there is always new material available. Students soon get used to using this system and develop good reading skills including:

- the ability to select reading materials according to a combination of degree of difficulty and degree of interest in the topic;
- dictionary skills;
- recording and reviewing the printouts they have read;
- re-using the language acquired in other contexts, for example in the pupils' own writing.

The idea is not new and was first developed using conventional authentic materials – magazines, comics, newspapers and brochures. However, the Internet provides a richer and more up-to-date source of material. Particular features include:

- pupils look forward to updated printouts from sites they have read previously;
- pupils are motivated to visit sites on-line.

Research for oral topic at A level and Higher Still
At this level teachers often encourage students to work independently and autonomously. If there is less emphasis on taught sessions and more on independent study, the use of the Internet is easily incorporated into the students' learning style. A set of Internet stations is needed in a readily accessible resources area such as the school library. A booking system is useful as a technical help to support students and to provide unobtrusive supervision to avoid misuse. Students can also be asked to sign a contract specifying that Internet access is for authorised study purposes only!

The modern languages department can develop a simple guide to using the Internet explaining the techniques and procedures to access the World Wide Web and providing information on recommended sites and how to search for sites in the various languages of study.

It is worth developing a system for collecting interesting sites and storing these on the computer so that students and teachers can recommend a site, perhaps with a very brief site description in the target language which can be produced by using language from the site itself. These sites should be checked and included in the list of interesting sites for each language – either in printed form or directly available on the computers, thereby avoiding re-typing of complex URLs.

Students can develop their Web skills during the A level or Higher Still course at the same time as enhancing their language skills. In lessons, there can be regular opportunities for oral presentations based on a visit to a website. Finally, students might use the Web to research for the oral topics.

News from the Web
The latest news from the Web can be displayed on a notice board in the languages area with printouts of a range of items:

- news stories from abroad including foreign coverage of home news;
- sports updates on events abroad – Tour de France, European football, Olympics;
- general interest – hedgehogs, Greenpeace, local festivals;
- home page of the week.

Naturally, it takes a lot of work to keep this up to date so the load needs to be shared between languages teachers, FLAs, student teachers and pupils, allocating responsibility for different languages and different topics.

From *WWW/The Internet*, InfoTech 3, CILT 1998.

The Internet is a good source of texts which we ignore at our peril. If we do not make use of the information revolution which is the Internet, MFL teachers will lose status in learners' eyes and lose standing in the school. The Internet has possibilities which are far reaching and important. The equivalent of ignoring it would be ignoring the arrival of the printing press. It is an influential resource and it is affecting the way learners learn.

SOME QUESTIONS ANSWERED FOR DEPARTMENTS SETTING UP A READING PROGRAMME

- ### *Should all learners and teachers be involved?*
  Where possible it is advisable that the establishment of a reading scheme should involve all members of a department. This may require careful presentation of the idea and some negotiation. Though a teacher working in isolation could indeed, given the resources, establish a class library, maximum advantage for learning will be gained from teachers working together. This will mean that developmental ideas can be shared and issues of progression and continuity can be addressed.

- ### *Should there be a dedicated reading period?*
  This will depend on the time and resources available. It may be that you have enough resources to run a loan scheme so that much of the reading can be done at home. This is an unlikely scenario for many schools, however, and reading for pleasure will need to be planned into the scheme of work. Though such work can be implemented on an ad hoc basis, if it is to have status in learners' eyes it needs to be seen as a departmental priority. This will only happen if the reading 'period' happens on a regular basis. The most efficient way to organise this, where several classes and teachers are involved with a limited range of shared resources, will be to instigate a reading period which might take place once, twice or three times per month for each class or for certain years.

- ### *How often should we have a reading period?*
  Reading periods should be short and frequent. A period of 35 minutes every two weeks will be the maximum possible for many departemnts, due to other pressures on curriculum time.

- ### *Where will the reading period take place?*
  This will depend on the facilities available. The library would be an ideal place, but this might not be feasible in a large school or in a department where all classes will be having reading periods over the course of a fortnight or a month. It may well be that reading resources are kept in 'Book Boxes' which are moved from room to room and the reading period takes place in the normal classroom. Ideally, however, learners should be in a quiet and comfortable area not necessarily associated with their day-to-day languages lessons.

- ***Should we have multiple copies of popular books?***
  Yes. This will be particularly important in schools where there are sufficient resources to allow books to be taken out on loan.

- ***Where are the books to be housed?***
  Ideally in the school library since they will then be classified along with other books and will fall under the jurisdiction of the librarian or person in charge of the library. This will save time for the department but will also demonstrate to learners that foreign language books have the same status as other books. However, this may not be an ideal location for some departments in which case books will need to be stored along with other departmental resources, with easy access for all teachers and learners.

- ***Should learners be set targets, e.g. one book per term?***
  It is useful to set targets for learners. However, these must be realistic and teachers need to be consistent in making sure that learners achieve them.

- ***Will learners select books for themselves?***
  Ideally, yes, though teachers or other learners may wish to give some guidance on appropriate levels. Learners may also need guidance on content in order to make their choice.

- ***Do learners need to record what is read?***
  Not necessarily, but a sense of achievement can be gained if a record of reading is built up. Such a record could also be used for formal or informal assessment purposes. However, the department needs to think through the purpose of the reading period. The very act of linking it to formal assessment can destroy the sense of pleasure which it may hope to engender in learners

- ***How much time shall we need for planning?***
  This will depend on the resources already available and the commitment of teachers. If new resources have to be selected and bought and a system for operating the reading programme has to be put in place, then this could take up to a year to get fully organised, given the other responsibilities of teachers in the department. However, a term could suffice if several teachers are involved and some resources are already in place or if an enthusiatic teacher with a low teaching commitment is enthusiastic and available.

CONCLUSION

And finally …

It is important to look to ourselves. Are we readers? Do we like reading? Are we in the habit of reading? Do we appreciate the benefits of reading in terms of our own foreign languages acquisition? The answer may be 'No, not really!'. The fault lies not necessarily in ourselves, as we work under pressure and are more and more accountable to external agencies such as OFSTED. But pupils will find it difficult to catch the reading bug unless the department has it! It is important that learners have positive role models, seeing their teachers as foreign language readers. Developing reading in the classroom, however, is not an individual but a group task. Teachers need to work together to think through their approach to texts for reading for pleasure. If this can be a part of an in-service programme, either in school, between schools or across a borough or a county, then so much the better. We have made progress in the last ten years. We now need to revisit this aspect of teaching and learning to develop fresh ideas and innovative approaches. I hope that this Pathfinder will act as a catalyst for teachers' creative thinking in this important area.

Appendix 1: References

Atkinson T, InfoTech3: *WWW: the Internet* (CILT, 1998)

Byrne D, *Focus on the classroom* (Modern English Publications, 1998)

Buzan T, *The speed reading book* (BBC Books, 1997)

Carrell P L in Carrell P, J Devine and D E Eskey (eds), *Interactive approaches to second language reading* (Cambridge, 1988)

Clarke M A and S Silberstein, 'Towards a realisation of psycho-linguistic principles in the ESL reading class' in *Language Learning* 27:1 (1977)

Gardiner J R, *Stone fox* (Harper Trophy, 1980)

Hawkins E, Study Guide E887 Open University PGCE (Open University Press, 1993)

Krashen S and T Terrell, *The natural approach. Language acquisition in the classroom* (Prentice Hall International English Language Teaching, 1983)

Little D, S Devitt and D Singleton, *Learning foreign languages from authentic texts: theory and practice* (Authentik/CILT, 1989)

Goodman K S, 'Psycholinguistic universals in the reading process' in Pimsleur P and T Quinn (eds), *The psychology of second language learning* (Cambridge University Press, 1971)

Gowan P and M Turner, 'Raising reading attainment in modern languages' in Swarbrick A, (ed), *Teaching modern languages* (Routledge, 1994)

Grabe W, 'Current developments in second language reading research' in *TESOL Quarterly* 25:3, 375–406 (1991)

Horsenfeld C, 'Case studies of ninth grade readers' in Anderson C and A H Urquhart, *Reading in a foreign language* (Longman, 1984)

Lundahl B, *Autentiska engelsksprakiga barn- och ungdoms-böcker på mellanstadiet* (Malmö: Lärarhogskolan, 1994)

Lundahl B, '"Den var bra. Har du en till likaden?" Autentiska texter i allman kurs engelska pa högstadiet' in *Amnesdidaktiska studier* nr 5 (Malmö: Lärarhögskolan, 1995)

Macaro E, 'Learner strategies: piloting awareness and training' in *Tuttitalia* (September 1998)

Nuttall C, *Teaching reading skills in a foreign language* (Heinemann Educational Books, 1985)

Palmberg R, 'On lexical inferencing and the young foreign language learner' in *System* 15:1, 69–76 (1987)

Rendall H, Pathfinder 33: *Stimulating grammatical awareness* (CILT, 1998)

Taylor A, Pathfinder 9: *Languages home and away* (CILT, 1991)

Williams R, 'Top 10 principles for teaching reading' in *ELT Journal* 40:1 (Oxford University Press, 1986)

Appendix 2: Useful publishers' addresses

Authentik Learning Resources Ltd
27 Westland Square
Dublin 2
Ireland
Tel: Freephone UK 0800 387027

Longman
Freepost Addison Wesley Longman
Schools Division
Harlow
Essex CM20 2YF
Tel: Freephone 0800 579579

Stanley Thornes
Ellenborough House
Wellington St
Cheltenham
Glos GL50 1YW
Tel: 01242 267275

Thomas Nelson and Sons Ltd
Nelson House
Mayfield Rd
Walton on Thames
Surrey
KT12 5PL
Tel: 01264 342992

Hodder and Stoughton Educational
Direct Services
78 Milton Park
Abingdon
Oxon OX14 4TD
Tel: 01235 400405

Collins Educational
Harper Collins Publishers
Westerhill Rd
Bishopbriggs
Glasgow G64 2QT
Tel: 0141 306 3573 or 0141 306 3171

Oxford University Press
Educational Supply Section
Saxon Way West
Corby
Northants NN18 9ES
Tel: 01536 741171

Heinemann
School/College orders dept
Heinemann Educational
Freepost
PO Box 381
Oxford OX2 8BR
Tel: 01865 314320

European Schoolbooks Ltd
Head Office and Warehouse
The Runnings
Cheltenham
Glos GL51 9PQ
Tel: 01242 245252

The European Bookshop
5 Warwick St
London W1R 5RA
Tel: 020 7734 5259

Appendix 3: Comenius Centres in the UK

The Birmingham Comenius Centre
Co-ordinator: Pete Lawton
Martineau Centre, Balden Road, Harborne,
Birmingham B32 2EH
Tel: 0121 303 1190. Fax: 0121 303 1179
E-mail: pete-lawton@birmingham.gov.uk

The Bristol & West of England Comenius Centre
(a three-site centre)
Co-ordinator: Ian Gathercole
Resources Centre, School of Education, University
of Bristol, 35 Berkeley Square, Bristol BS8 1JA
Tel: 0117 928 7021. Fax: 0117 928 7110
E-mail: ian.gathercole@bristol.ac.uk
with
Co-ordinators: Mary Ryan and John Budd
Bristol Education Centre, Sheridan Road, Horfield,
Bristol BS7 0PU
Tel: 0117 931 1111. Fax: 0117 931 1619
and with
Co-ordinator: Irene Wilkie
Faculty of Languages and European Studies,
University of the West of England, Coldharbour
Road, Frenchay, Bristol BS16 1QY
Tel: 0117 965 6261 ext. 2393. Fax: 0117 976 3843
E-mail: Irene.Wilkie@uwe.ac.uk

The Greater Manchester Comenius Centre
Co-ordinator: Adalgisa Serio
Manchester College of Arts & Technology, City
Centre Campus, Lower Hardman Street,
Manchester M3 3ER
Tel: 0161 953 2266. Fax: 0161 953 2259

The Homerton Comenius Centre
Co-ordinator: Barry Jones
Homerton College, Cambridge CB2 2PH
Tel: 01223 507111. Fax: 01223 507120
E-mail: blj20@cam.ac.uk
Enquiries to:
Sheena Sturrock, Administrator
Tel/answerphone/fax: 01223 507257
E-mail: sms29@cam.ac.uk

The Leicestershire Comenius Centre
Co-ordinator: Pam Haezewindt
Quorn Hall, Meynell Road, Quorn, Loughborough
LE12 8BG
Tel: 01509 416990. Fax: 01509 416993
E-mail: pam@leics-comenius.org.uk
Website: http://www.leics-comenius.org.uk

The North East Comenius Centre
Co-ordinator: Phil Drabble
Broadway Centre for Educational Development,
Springwell Road, Sunderland SR4 8NW
Tel: 0191 553 5600. Fax: 0191 553 5633
E-mail: phil.drabble@sunderland.gov.uk

The North West Comenius Centre
(a two-site centre)
Co-ordinator: James Burch
Languages Development Centre, St Martin's
College,
Bowerham Road, Lancaster LA1 3JD
E-mail: j.burch@ucsm.ac.uk
Enquiries to: Carolyn Lucas, Administrator
Tel: 01524 384488. Fax: 01524 384492
E-mail: c.lucas@ucsm.ac.uk
Website:
http://www.blackburn.ac.uk/comenius/welcome.html
with
Co-ordinator: Chris Jenkins
Blackburn College, Feilden Street,
Blackburn BB2 1LH
Tel: 01254 292196. Fax: 01254 682700
E-mail: c.jenkins@blackburn.ac.uk
Administrator: Beryl Hewlett
E-mail: b.hewlett@blackburn.ac.uk

The Oxford Comenius Centre
Co-ordinator: Hilary Lowe
Westminster College, Oxford OX2 9AT
Tel: 01865 253551. Fax: 01865 247644
E-mail: h.lowe@ox-west.ac.uk

CILT

The Southampton & Hampshire Comenius Centre
(a two-site centre)
Co-ordinators: Dr Michael Grenfell (Secretary)
Tel: 023 8059 3472. Fax: 023 8059 3556
E-mail: m.grenfell@soton.ac.uk
with
Bob Thomas (Chair)
Tel: 023 9244 1459. Fax: 023 9249 8174
E-mail: ediahtbt@hants.gov.uk
University site: The Hartley Library, The University
of Southampton, University Road, Southampton
SO17 1BJ
Administrator: Paul Boagey
Tel: 023 8059 2180
Hampshire LEA site:
Fort Hill Community School, Kenilworth Road,
Basingstoke RG23 8JQ
Administrator: Barbara Band
Tel: 01256 354311

The Trinity & All Saints Comenius Centre, Leeds
Co-ordinator: Simon Green
Trinity & All Saints College, Brownberrie Lane,
Horsforth, Leeds LS18 5HD
E-mail: s.green@tasc.ac.uk
Enquiries to: Brenda Pease, Administrator
Tel: 0113 283 7226. Fax: 0113 283 7226
E-mail: b.pease@tasc.ac.uk

The West Country Comenius Centre
(a two-site centre)
Co-ordinators:
Geoff Grigg
Cornwall LEA, CCED
E-mail: ggrigg@rmplc.co.uk
with
*Chris Wakely, Adviser for Modern Foreign
Languages*
Devon Curriculum Services, Great Moor House,
Bittern Road, Sowton, Exeter EX2 7NL
Tel: 01392 384361. Fax: 01392 384880
E-mail: cwakely@dial.devon-cc.gov.uk
and with
Annie Singer, Adviser for MFL
Education Development Service, County Hall,
Taunton TA1 4DY
Tel: 01823 356 266. Fax: 01823 330598
E-mail: amsinger@somerset.gov.uk

Resource bases:
Exeter Schools' Centre, Summerway Middle School,
Summerway, Exeter EX4 8DF
Administrator: Ann Roberts
Tel: 01392 464986. Fax: 01392 460655
and
Cornwall Centre of Educational Development
(CCED), Penhaligon Building, Trevenson Lane,
Pool, Redruth TR15 3RG
Tel: 01209 616947/6. Fax: 01209 616949

The West Sussex Comenius Centre
Co-ordinator: Anne Feltham
Tel: 01293 435651. Fax: 01293 435601
E-mail: anne.feltham@westsussex.gov.uk
Director of Resource Base: Candy Newman
Tel: 01243 532970. Fax: 01243 531080
E-mail: candy.newman@westsussex.gov.uk
Resource centre:
Southern Area Professional Centre, Glebeside
Avenue,
Worthing BN14 7PR
Administrator: Sîan Prior
Tel: 01903 847625. Fax: 01903 847601
E-mail: comenius@westsussex.gov.uk

The Yorkshire Rose Comenius Centre
Co-ordinator: David Stork
East Riding of Yorkshire Council
Department of Education, Leisure & Libraries
County Hall, Beverley HU17 9BA
Tel: 01482 885370
E-mail: davld.stork@east-riding-of-yorkshire.gov.uk
Main resources base:
Wolfreton School, Southells Way, Kirk Ella,
East Riding of Yorkshire HU10 7LU
Administrator: Heather Hodgson
Tel: (direct) 01482 658485
or (Wolfreton School) 01482 659356/7/8/9
Opening hours: Monday, Wednesday and Thursday
09.15-13.15, Tuesday 12.00-17.30
Other resource collections
York
The College Library, University College of Ripon
and York St John, Lord Mayor's Walk, York YO31
7EX
North Yorkshire
Northallerton College, Northallerton, North Yorkshire
(contact the Resources Manager)